Time to try.... the ANTI-LECTIN Diet

Lectin-Free Recipes To Help Heal Your Gut, Lose Weight & Reduce Inflammation

CookNation

Time to try... The ANTI-LECTIN Diet

Lectin-Free Recipes To Help Heal Your Gut, Lose Weight & Reduce Inflammation

ISBN 978-1-912511-57-0

DISCLAIMER

This book is designed to provide information on the popular Plant Paradox/Anti-Lectin Diet . Some recipes may contain nuts or traces of nuts. Those suffering from any allergies associated with nuts should avoid any recipes containing nuts or nut based oils.
This information is provided and sold with the knowledge that the publisher and author do not offer any legal or other professional advice.
In the case of a need for any such expertise consult with the appropriate professional.
This book does not contain all information available on the subject, and other sources of recipes are available.
Every effort has been made to make this book as accurate as possible. However, there may be typographical and or content errors. Therefore, this book should serve only as a general guide and not as the ultimate source of subject information.
This book contains information that might be dated and is intended only to educate and entertain.
The author and publisher shall have no liability or responsibility to any person or entity regarding any loss or damage incurred, or alleged to have incurred, directly or indirectly, by the information contained in this book.

CONTENTS

INTRODUCTION

We spend much of our time learning about all the foods we should be eating; the nutrition they contain, whether they have superfood status and how they will help us be as healthy as we can be. However, The Plant Paradox has arrived and with it, a whole new way of thinking and it certainly will stop you in your tracks.

Dr Stephen Gundry; a cardiothoracic surgeon, professor, Director of The California Heart and Lung Institute and previously, an overweight, stressed individual decided to change his focus and start his own revolution.

Instead of concentrating on the foods we should be eating to improve our health and eradicate health complaints in the future, he began to study the foods we shouldn't eat and began a new thought process..... maybe the foods we are already eating are the problem?

Dr Gundry began to theorise that human evolution hadn't quite caught up with the foods around us. Before animals, insects and humans arrived on our planet, the plants had the run of the land. Nothing could harm them, and they had developed a strong sustainability programme with the natural desire to reproduce, their offspring were safe, and the ever-changing seasons were the root of their survival.

When insects and animals came along and considered plants to be a rather tasty way to survive, these plants had to evolve, they had to protect themselves and so began the production of lectins. In short, these are a long-term defence strategy that makes these plants and their offspring toxic, unpleasant and yielding the ability to make consumers rather unwell.

So, you may wonder how this information is coming to light now. Surely, we have been around for a while now and mother nature would have allowed our bodies to adapt to these changes and so-called lectins?

Unfortunately, we have moved a long a little quicker than mother nature, literally; she hadn't banked on us setting sail in boats no doubt! Grains such as corn, chia, quinoa, potatoes and other lectin rich foods never to reach our shores before, were discovered and grown in new soils in non-native countries. Traditional cooking methods that were used to protect against lectins were sometimes lost when these foods travelled about. These old-world cooking methods included soaking and removing the seeds, hulls and peels from plants where the main lectins resided.

When these lectins are not removed from foods we are consuming, our microbiome (the good bacteria in your body that brings about good health) becomes under attack. These lectins act as "bullies" and create holes in our gut wall defences, allowing unwanted waste products to escape and to potentially cause a number of health problems. This condition is known as a leaky gut and symptoms can vary from mild to severe.

With these "bullies" invading our bodies, our immune system gets a little confused. It can start attacking not just these lectins, but also healthy cells and tissues and that's when a number of auto-immune conditions can develop. Rheumatoid arthritis, Crohn's Disease, MS, celiac disease, psoriasis, lupus, IBS and Type 1 Diabetes are examples of these auto-immune conditions.

Dr Gundry is a firm believer in the leaky gut issues and reports that he has watched his patients improve their symptoms and sometimes resolve auto-immune conditions by following an anti-lectin diet. There is a large amount of information available to study and read on this subject and if you are suffering with an auto-immune condition, it's really worth a read!

Other points that Dr Gundry has made in his theories, are that there are also a number of other factors that make our bodies unable to process lectins and these are really worth thinking about –

- Our bodies are originally programmed to eat seasonally. This means we are adapted to eat ripe fruit in the warmer months, storing fat and preparing for a winter of lower calories. Our bodies then switch to start burning the stored fats during the winter and we are no longer eating fruits that are busy growing and re-producing for the next season. Air miles and freight suddenly makes fruit and vegetables of most kind, available all year round.

- We have been educated to believe that vegetables oils and whole grains are better alternatives. Traditionally, bread and pasta have been made using wheat that has been stripped of lectin-rich bran coats, this was the staple diet of many; white bread, white pasta, white rice. However, in this move to become "healthier", the whole grain varieties we are eating more of are actually packing more lectins in to our diet!

- We are also consuming more soy, wheat and corn via meat, dairy and wheat products. Cattle and poultry are fed large amounts of these (and anti-biotics!) and these are then transferred in to the products that we consume; which equals more lectins.

- Medications we reach for regularly also interfere with our bodies and their ability to manage lectins. Antacids reduce stomach acid, which is essential for your body to neutralise harmful bacteria. Anti-biotics and non-steroidal anti-inflammatory drugs also affect the microbiome and our healthy gut bacteria.

- Dr Gundry also highlights the endocrine disruptors that are found in the everyday plastics and chemicals we are open to, such as cling film, household cleaners, food packaging and toiletries. These play havoc with our body's processing, the liver is put under more stress, excess hormones can't be converted to vitamin D and this results in a number of other conditions, such as thyroid problems, osteoporosis, some cancer, Alzheimer's and dementia. Vitamin D also maintains the wall of your stomach and is an important nutrient for a leaky gut.

- Genetically modified foods and herbicides surrounding the production of grains, soy, beans, legumes, oats and corn are all consumed in high amounts when we are filling our diets with these food items and these lectins are harmful.

- And lastly, Dr Gundry points out some thoughts around days and nights. When we have long days and short nights, our body is programmed to switch to "fat store" mode, thinking winter is coming. With many of us sitting in front of a white screen for many hours, working, your body thinks it's summer all year round and won't shift extra fat.

So, there are a lot of theories as to why lectins can cause a number of medical conditions, with obesity and auto-immune disease being quite valid considerations. But just how easy is it to follow a lectin free diet to see if your body finds resolve from troublesome symptoms, excess weight that won't shift or an auto-immune condition?

The recipes in this book are here to motivate you to make an easy switch to a lectin-free life. Focussing on the foods you can eat will help you understand how Dr Gundry's approach isn't about starving you or eliminating all of your favourite foods. Adapting your cooking methods may allow you to re-introduce some foods and persevering will allow you to celebrate a new "you", where you will begin to look forward to and celebrate all the foods you can eat.

How Do You Do It?

There is a 3-step process to beginning The Plant Paradox, lectin-free diet. Once you reach step 3 you will have a huge selection of foods available to enjoy. No food group needs to be avoided andyou will be educated to shop better and make better choices.

Phase 1

YES, YOU CAN EAT

- **Organic vegetables (not included in the Do Not Eat)**
- **Avocado, asparagus, celery**
- **Fresh herbs**
- **Olives**
- **Avocado, macadamia, walnut, hemp seed oils and ghee (clarified butter)**
- **One small portion of wild caught fish or pasture fed chicken**
- **Tempeh**
- **Hemp tofu**
- **Quorn products**
- **Shellfish**
- **Nuts (not almonds)**
- **Lemon juice, vinegar, mustard**
- **Green, black and herbal teas, coffee**
- **Stevia**

DO NOT EAT

- **Any grains (including the pseudo-grains such as quinoa)**
- **Any dairy**
- **No fruit**
- **No sugar**
- **No seeds**
- **No soy**
- **No nightshades (courgettes, tomatoes, etc.) roots or tubers**
- **No corn, soy or canola oils**
- **No beef or conventionally raised meats**

This Phase 1 should be followed for 3 days where your unfriendly gut bacteria will be starved, and you will be ready for Phase 2.

Phase 2

You can eat all the same things as in Phase 1, where you will continue to make your microbiome a happier environment..

In phase 2 you can add the following to your diet:

- **Pastured and omega 3 eggs**
- **Turnips, parsnips, celeriac, sweet potatoes, artichokes, okra, radicchio**
- **Shirataki noodles**
- **Green bananas and unripe mangoes and papaya**
- **Inulin and yacon syrups**
- **Almond, cassava and coconut flours**
- **Millet and sorghum**
- **Mushrooms**
- **Plain goats, sheep or coconut yoghurt**
- **Figs and dates**
- **Extra virgin oils and coconut oil (after 2 weeks)**

This repair and restore phase should continue for 6 weeks where you will be breaking down past bad habits and establishing new ones. You may start to feel better during this time, but it is essential that you don't go back to the bad habits and instead continue to nurture your gut bacteria and the new and improving microbiome.

Phase 3

It may be a case of re-introducing foods on this list, one at a time, to see if there are any effects on how you are feeling. Preparing these foods differently may enable you to continue eating them in the future or you may just find avoiding quite easy.

You can now start to eat :

- **All foods on Phase 1 and 2**
- **Peeled and de-seeded baby cucumbers, courgettes, aubergines, tomatoes (Heirloom variety are best)**
- **Pressure cooked beans, rice and lentils**
- **Casein A2 Cows milk**
- **White sourdough**

There are many foods to celebrate on a Lectin Free Diet once you have completed these phases. You could go straight to Phase 3 if you would like, but the rewards may take a little longer to take effect.
The foods on the YES list include the following and can be enjoyed freely going forward. The NO list should be avoided when you are undertaking an anti lectin lifestyle..

There are a handful of recipes here to see you through Phase 1 and then you can pick and choose through all the other recipes for Phases 2 & 3.

YES

Oils

- **Algae, olive, coconut, macadamia,**
- **MCT Red palm, rice bran oil, sesame oil, avocado, perilla, walnut,**
- **flavoured cod liver oil**

Sweeteners

- **stevia, inulin, yacon, monk fruit,**
- **xylitol and erythritol.**

Nuts and Seeds

- **Macadamia, walnuts, pistachios**

NO

Oils

- **Soy, grape-seed, corn, peanut,**
- **cottonseed, safflower, sunflower,**
- **partially hydrogenated, vegetable and**
- **canola**

Sweeteners

- **Agave, Splenda, NutraSweet, Diet Drinks**
- **Maltodextrin**

Nuts and Seeds

- **Pumpkin**

YES

- Pecans, coconuts and their products,
- Hazelnuts, chestnuts, brazil nuts, pine nuts,
- Flaxseeds, hemp seeds and protein powder,
- Psyllium, sesame seeds

- All Olives

- Dark Chocolate (72% cocoa)

- Vinegars (all without sugar)

- All Herbs

Flour and Grains
- Coconut, almond, hazelnut, sesame,
- chestnuts, cassava, tiger nut, arrowroot,
- sorghum, millet, tapioca (cassava)

Dairy
- A2 (A1 Casein mutation free)
- Buffalo and goat products
- French/Italian Cheese and Butters
- (naturally A1 free)
- Whey protein powder
- Cheese from Switzerland
- Organic sour cream, heavy cream and cream cheese
- Clarified butter (ghee)
- Parmigiana-Reggiano

Fruits (no juices) IN SEASON
- All berries,
- Pears, apples,
- Pomegranate, kiwis
- Citrus
- Nectarines and peaches
- Passionfruit
- Plums, apricots
- Figs, dates

Vegetables
- All cruciferous (broccoli, cauliflower, bok choi, cabbage, rocket, etc.)
- Celery, onion, garlic, leeks, chives,

NO

- Sunflower
- Chia
- Peanut
- Cashews

- No chilli flakes or miso

Flour and Grains
- No wheat flours, pseudo-grain flours,
- oat, no corn products, popcorn, barley, rice, bulgur, quinoa, rye

Dairy
- All dairy from normal cows

(including cheese and yoghurts)
- Ice cream
- Kefir
- Ricotta, cottage cheese, butter
- Frozen Yoghurt
- Cream
- Fromage Frais and Crème Fraice

Fruits
- Cucumbers, courgettes, aubergine
- Pumpkins, squashes, melons, goji berries
- Tomatoes, peppers, chilli (At phase 3 you can gently introduce tomatoes, peppers & chilli you can back to your diet in small amounts if there are no adverse affects. Make sure you remove the seeds and skin.

Vegetables
- Peas, legumes, chickpeas, beans,
- Edamame, lentils, soy, green beans, tofu, sugar snap peas, potatoes

• Carrots (raw) • Beetroot • Radishes • Artichoke • Herbs • Asparagus Mushrooms • Leafy Greens and Salad Leaves • Sea vegetables • Parsnips • Celeriac • Sweet Potato • Tiger nuts, • Green Mango **Protein (small portions only)** • Chicken, turkey - pastured • Omega 3 and pastured eggs • Duck, goose, pheasant, quail, grouse • All grass fed - Wild game, venison, lamb, beef, pork and prosciutto • Hemp Tofu • Tempeh (grain free) • Quorn	**Protein** • Any farmed proteins that have not been raised on pasture.

Conclusion

There is a wealth of information on the internet about lectins, and there are other variations and opinions on them too. It is important to understand though, that we are all individuals and we all react differently to foods, so choosing your own lifestyle and approach is key to a successful change in the way you eat

This book is a guide to introduce you to the theory and broad principles of Lectin Free Living to help you find what works for YOU. Always consult your health care provider if you have medical conditions before embarking on change and also keep them informed of any negative results or worries.

The theory behind Dr Gundry's Plant Paradox is really worth investigating if you are interested in finding out more about lectins in our food and environment. There is a whole world of food out there to enjoy, to help us be the best we can, so educate yourself a bit further, understand your body and eat well; it deserves it.

CookNation

PLANT PARADOX

PHASE 1 RECIPES

ANTI-LECTIN

SERVES 1

BASIL AND LEMON SMOOTHIE

PHASE 1 RECIPES

Ingredients

- 1 avocado, stone removed and peeled
- 1 lemon, zest and juice
- 5 fresh basil leaves
- 250ml/8floz coconut milk

Method

1 Place the avocado, lemon, basil and milk into a high-speed blender.

2 Give it a shake and process until smooth.

3 Pour into a chilled glass and enjoy immediately.

CHEF'S NOTE

You need to look for filling recipes in phase 1 and this contains a whole avocado which will boost energy and provide some great monounsaturated fats to your diet.

SERVES 1

HEMP TOFU AND NORI CRUMBS

PHASE 1 RECIPES

Ingredients

- 1 tsp avocado oil
- 100g/3½oz hemp tofu (this can be made yourself)
- 1 tbsp nutritional yeast
- 50g/2oz kale, shredded
- 1 garlic clove, crushed
- ½ red onion, sliced
- 2 sheets of nori
- 1 tbsp lemon juice

Method

1 Place the sheets of nori in a hot oven for 5 minutes to crisp up. Chop finely and leave to one side.

2 Heat the oil in a large saucepan and add the hemp tofu. Cook this over a high heat to brown all over.

3 Reduce the heat and add the garlic, onion and celery. Stir for 4-5 minutes until starting to soften.

4 Add the kale, lemon juice and nutritional yeast and stir until the greens start to wilt.

5 Serve with the nori crumbs on top.

CHEF'S NOTE

Nutritional yeast is a great flavour friend in a lectin free diet. Not only does it bring a great savoury taste, it also provides a useful collection of B vitamins.

SERVES 1

OVEN ROASTED FENNEL AND PRAWN BAKE

PHASE 1 RECIPES

Ingredients

- 1 tsp white wine vinegar
- 1 tsp avocado oil
- 1 bok choi, shredded
- ¼ large fennel, root removed and sliced
- 75g/3oz cooked prawns
- 1-2 sprigs of dill
- 1 tsp salt
- 1tsp lemon zest to serve

Method

1 Pre-heat the oven to 200°C/Gas Mark 6 and cut a large piece of baking paper.

2 In a small bowl, mix the oil, vinegar and salt.

3 In the middle of the baking paper, place the bok choi, fennel and pile the prawns on, followed by the dill.

4 Fold the baking paper over the ingredients and start to fold in the edges, pleating, to form a semi-circle.

5 Leave one part open and pour in the oil and vinegar. Seal completely.

6 Place in the oven and bake for 10 minutes until the vegetable are softened.

7 Grate over some lemon zest to serve.

CHEF'S NOTE

This form of cooking is called en-papillote, which means to "cook and serve in a paper bag". It's a healthy way to cook and you can add fish, chicken and many different vegetables for a great prepare ahead meal.

SERVES 2

WATERCRESS, CELERY AND LEEK SOUP

PHASE 1 RECIPES

Ingredients

- 1 tbsp almond oil
- 1 onion, diced
- 1 garlic clove, diced
- 1 stick of celery, diced
- 200g/7oz watercress, tough stems removed
- 1 leek, shredded
- 2 celery stalks, chopped
- Small bunch of fresh thyme
- 600ml/1 pint vegetable stock
- 1 tsp salt

Method

1. Heat the oil in a saucepan and add the onion and garlic.
2. Stir over a medium heat for 4-5 minutes until softened.
3. Add the celery and leek and cook for a further 5-6 minutes.
4. Add the stock, salt, thyme and watercress and simmer for 15 minutes or until all of the vegetables are soft.
5. Using a stick blender or food processor blend until smooth.

CHEF'S NOTE

Watercress contains more vitamin C than an orange and more calcium than milk. It provides vitamins A, B6, B12, iron and magnesium and is a great plant to be eating on Phase 1.

SERVES 1

CHICKEN, OLIVE AND ROCKET SALAD

PHASE 1 RECIPES

Ingredients

- 1 chicken breast, cooked and shredded
- 4-5 black or green olives, chopped
- 1 celery stick, sliced
- 100g/3½oz rocket leaves
- Small bunch of flat leaf parsley, roughly chopped
- ½ avocado, stone removed, peeled & sliced
- 1 tbsp avocado oil
- ¼ tsp mustard
- 1 tsp white wine vinegar
- ½ tsp salt
- 1 tbsp lemon juice
- 1 tbsp lemon zest

Method

1 Mix the lemon zest, juice, salt, mustard, oil and vinegar together and set aside.

2 Toss the chicken, olives, celery, rocket, parsley and avocado together and place in a bowl to serve.

3 Drizzle over the lemon and mustard dressing and serve.

CHEF'S NOTE

When choosing chicken for a lectin-free diet, be sure to buy the pasture raised poultry. These chickens aren't fed on corn, so the meat will be free of lectins.

PLANT PARADOX

PHASE 2 & 3 BREAKFAST

ANTI-LECTIN

SERVES 1

RASPBERRY AND VANILLA BREAKFAST CAKE

BREAKFAST PHASE 2 RECIPES

Ingredients

- 2 tbsp extra-virgin olive oil (after 2 weeks of Phase 2)
- 1 tbsp coconut flour
- 1 tbsp almond flour
- 1 tsp stevia
- ½ tsp baking power
- ½ tsp vanilla extract
- 1 egg, beaten
- 1 tbsp raspberries

Method

1 Beat the oil, flours, stevia, baking powder, vanilla and egg together in a mug until smooth.

2 Gently fold in the raspberries

3 Place in a microwave for 1 minute 30 seconds, or until risen, cooked and soft.

CHEF'S NOTE

It is best to eat fruits that are in season when following an anti-lectin diet so you get the best nutrition possible.

SERVES 1

BLUEBERRY & CINNAMON BREAKFAST CAKE

BREAKFAST
PHASE
2
RECIPES

Ingredients

- 2 tbsp extra-virgin olive oil (after 2 weeks of Phase 2)
- 1 tbsp coconut flour
- 1 tbsp almond flour
- ½ tsp cinnamon
- 2 tsp coconut sugar
- ½ tsp baking powder
- 1 egg
- 1 tbsp blueberries

Method

1 Beat the oil, flours, stevia, baking powder, cinnamon and egg together in a mug until smooth.

2 Gently fold in the blueberries

3 Place in a microwave for 1 minute 30 seconds, until risen, cooked and soft.

CHEF'S NOTE

These breakfast mug cakes are a great breakfast for when you are short of time. Add whatever fruits and spices you like.

SERVES 4

HOT BUTTERED CINNAMON PANCAKES

BREAKFAST
PHASE 2
RECIPES

Ingredients

- 125g/4oz of cassava flour
- 1 ½ tbsp stevia
- 1 tbsp baking powder
- 1 tsp ground cinnamon
- 2 eggs
- 3 tbsp avocado oil
- 250ml/8½floz cup milk (goats/almond/coconut)
- 60ml/2floz cup cold water
- 6 tsp almond butter for serving

Method

1 Whisk all of the ingredients together (exept the almond butter) until smooth.

2 Leave the mixture to sit f0r 20 minutes.

3 Heat a non-stick frying pan.

4 Pour tablespoons of the mix into the pan and cook for 2-3 minutes on both sides until golden and risen.

5 Serve with softened butter.

CHEF'S NOTE

Stevia is a natural product and a good sweetener to use on a Lectin-Free diet. It's a herb that is actually 3 times sweeter than sugar, so use sparingly.

SPINACH SCRAMBLED EGGS

SERVES 1

BREAKFAST
PHASE
2
RECIPES

Ingredients

- 2 eggs, beaten
- 1 tsp milk (goat/almond/coconut)
- 100g/3½oz baby spinach leaves
- ½ tsp sea salt
- 1 tsp dried thyme
- Millet bread and butter to serve

Method

1 Beat the eggs and milk together and pour in to a small saucepan.

2 Stir continually over a medium heat until the eggs start to scramble.

3 When the first lumps appear, roughly tear the spinach leaves and add to the pan.

4 Continue to stir until the spinach is wilted and the eggs are just set, but not dry.

5 Toast the millet bread if you like and add some butter.

6 Serve the eggs immediately.

CHEF'S NOTE

You could add a tsp of nut butter to the eggs instead of the milk to make a richer breakfast, both options create a lovely soft scramble.

SERVES 1

BAKED EGGS, HERBS AND AVOCADO

BREAKFAST PHASE 2 RECIPES

Ingredients

- 2 eggs
- Handful of baby spinach
- 2 tbsp flat leaf parsley
- ½ an avocado

Method

1 Pre-heat the oven to 220°C/Gas Mark 7 and grease a small/medium ramekin.

2 Dice and chop the spainch, parsely and avocado.

3 Place the spinach, parsley and avocado on the bottom evenly.

4 Crack the eggs, carefully on top and place in the oven for 8-10 minutes until set.

CHEF'S NOTE

Spinach is a great source of vitamins A, C and K and multiple minerals, such as magnesium, calcium and iron.

SERVES 1

MUSHROOM AND TRUFFLE BAKED EGGS

BREAKFAST
PHASE
2
RECIPES

Ingredients

- 2 eggs
- 2-3 drops of truffle oil (after 2 weeks of phase 2)
- 50g/2oz chestnut mushrooms, sliced

Method

1 Pre-heat the oven to 220˚C/Gas Mark 7 and grease a small/medium ramekin.

2 Place the mushrooms on the bottom evenly and drizzle the truffle oil on top.

3 Crack the eggs, carefully, on top and place in the oven for 8-10 minutes until set.

CHEF'S NOTE

Find a truffle oil that's made from cold pressed extra virgin olive oil and a good quality one. This oil should only be used to dress dishes and not to cook with and will bring a unique, luxurious flavour to food.

SERVES 2

FRUIT SALAD WITH A LEMON AND MINT DRIZZLE

BREAKFAST PHASE 2 RECIPES

Ingredients

- 2 pears, cored and sliced lengthways
- 1 red skinned apple, cored and thinly sliced
- 2 kiwis, peeled and thinly sliced
- 7-8 red or green grapes, cut in half.
- 3 tbp lemon juice
- 1 tsp fresh mint, finely chopped

Method

1 Place the fruit onto two plates, in a pretty pattern.

2 Mix the lemon juice and mint leaves together.

3 Drizzle over the fruit and serve immediately.

CHEF'S NOTE

You could add a little yacon syrup or inulin to the lemon drizzle if you would like a little more sweetness.

SERVES 4

CHOCOLATE CHIP PANCAKES

BREAKFAST
PHASE
2&3
RECIPES

Ingredients

- 2 eggs
- 1 tsp vanilla extract
- 1 tbsp avocado oil
- 3 tsp stevia
- 140g/4½oz coconut yoghurt (or goat's milk yoghurt)
- 25g/1oz cup tapioca flour
- 25g/1oz cup coconut flour
- 25g/1oz cup almond flour
- 1 tsp baking powder
- 40g/1½oz cup of dark chocolate chips (72% cocoa at least)

Method

1 Beat all of the ingredients together and leave the mixture to one side for 20 minutes.

2 Add a little more yoghurt or milk if the mix becomes a little too thick due to the coconut flour.

3 Pour tablespoons of the mix on to a pre-heated non-stick frying pan.

4 Cook for 2-3 minutes on both sides, until it s cooked through and the chocolate is oozing.

CHEF'S NOTE

Make sure you use a dark chocolate for this recipe that is free of soy lecithin and only made with natural ingredients and low sugar.

SERVES 4

CHEESY WAFFLES

BREAKFAST
PHASE
2&3
RECIPES

Ingredients

- 100g/3½oz almond flour
- ½ tbsp baking powder
- 250ml/8½floz coconut milk
- 2 tbsp avocado oil
- 3 eggs
- 2 + 1 tbsp parmigiana-reggiano

Method

1 Pre-heat a waffle iron.

2 Whisk the ingredients together (apart from 1 tbsp of the cheese) until smooth.

3 Pour into the waffle iron, as per the instructions and cook until all of the batter is used up.

4 Heat a grill and sprinkle the reserved cheese over the top of the waffles. Heat them under the hot grill, until the cheese is crisp and golden.

CHEF'S NOTE

Always ensure you are using the unsweetened versions of non-dairy milk.

SERVES 1

ROCKET AND HERB OMELETTE

BREAKFAST
PHASE
2&3
RECIPES

Ingredients

- 3 eggs
- 1 tbsp chopped chives
- 1 tbsp chopped flat leaf parsley
- 50g/2oz rocket leaves
- 1 tbsp avocado oil

Method

1 Heat the oil in a frying pan.

2 Beat the eggs together well and pour into the hot oil. Swirl them around the pan until the bottom is beginning to set.

3 Scatter over the rocket and herbs, fold the omelette over and cook until the eggs are just set.

4 Serve immediately.

CHEF'S NOTE

Rocket is a lovely peppery, dark green salad leaf that packs a lot of flavour. It is full of Vitamins A, B, C and K and is very similar to the nutritional benefits of kale.

SERVES 2

BREAKFAST SALAD WITH ANCHOVIES

BREAKFAST
PHASE
2&3
RECIPES

Ingredients

- 5/6 small anchoviess
- 1 lemon, juice and zest
- 2 tbsp extra virgin olive oil
- 2 eggs,
- 75g/3oz baby spinach leaves
- 75g/3oz rocket leaves
- 4 tbsp grated raw carrot

Method

1 Hardboil the eggs, peel & chop. Leave to cool while you prepare the rest of the salad.

2 Chop the anchovies and spinach leaves

3 Toss all of the ingredients together until well combined.

4 Serve immediately.

CHEF'S NOTE

Anchovies are a great source of omega-3 and have a tasty salty flavour that is quite unique. Don't add too many or they could overpower a dish.

MINI BREAKFAST SEEDED ROLLS

SERVES 10

BREAKFAST
PHASE
2&3
RECIPES

Ingredients

- 275g/10oz almond flour
- 2 tsp salt
- 100g/3½oz tapioca starch
- 2 tsp baking powder
- 1 tsp stevia
- 2 tbsp hemp seeds
- 2 tbsp sesame seeds
- 2 tbsp white wine vinegar
- 120ml/4floz warm water
- 1 egg

Method

1 Pre-heat the oven to 200°C/Gas Mark 6 and grease a baking tray.

2 Boil a large pan of water.

3 Mix the flour, salt, tapioca, baking powder, seeds and stevia together.

4 Beat the eggs into the mix and add the warm water and vinegar. Briefly mix to combine well.

5 Shaped into 10 rolls and place in the boiling water. Simmer for 1 minute.

6 Place on the baking tray and bake for 10-12 minutes, until risen and brown.

7 When cooked and cooled a little, slice and fill with whatever filling you like.

CHEF'S NOTE

This is a wonderful recipe for a gluten free roll that has a chewy texture, similar to a bagel. The seeds add a good omega-3 boost to the recipe and also some energy to start the day.

SERVES 1

GOATS CHEESE EGG BAKES

BREAKFAST
PHASE
2&3
RECIPES

Ingredients

- 2 eggs, beaten
- 2 tbsp soft goats cheese
- 2 spring onions, shredded
- 1 tbsp chopped walnuts

Method

1 Pre-heat the oven to 200°C/Gas Mark 6 and grease 2 holes in a muffin pan.

2 Beat the eggs and goats cheese together until smooth. Pour in the muffin holes.

3 Drop the onions and walnuts into the egg mix and bake in the oven for 10-12 minutes until set.

CHEF'S NOTE

Goats cheese is safe to add to a lectin free diet and it is easier to digest than many dairy products. It is full of useful vitamins and it's a great probiotic to enhance gut health.

SERVES 1

SUMMER FRUIT BOWL

BREAKFAST
PHASE
2&3
RECIPES

Ingredients

- 3 tbsp blueberries
- 2 tbsp raspberries
- 4-5 strawberries, halved
- 2 tbsp coconut yoghurt
- ½ grated apple and 1 tsp hemp seeds to top

Method

1. Place the fruits in a small bowl, either mixing them or making a section design to keep colours together.
2. Place the yoghurt on the top.
3. Add the grated apple and the hemp seeds over the yoghurt and enjoy immediately.

CHEF'S NOTE

Eat berries and other fruits in moderation as part of a lectin free diet, and always eat when they are in season. The added hemp seed here will help balance blood sugars and will add a lovely nutty texture that's full of protein.

SERVES 2

SORGHUM PORRIDGE

BREAKFAST PHASE 2&3 RECIPES

Ingredients

- 75g/3oz sorghum (grains not flour)
- 500ml/17floz coconut milk/goats milk/ almond milk
- 1 tbsp yacon syrup (or other sweetener of choice)
- 1 tsp ground cinnamon
- ½ tsp nutmeg
- 1 tsp coconut oil
- 1 tbsp yacon syrup
- 2 tbsp pecans, chopped

Method

1 Soak the sorghum overnight in plenty of water. Drain and then place the sorghum in a pan with the milk, sweetener and spices.

2 Simmer over a very low heat for roughly 1 hour, until cooked and soft. Add a little more milk or water of it becomes a little dry.

3 Divide between two bowls and top with the chopped pecans and yacon syrup.

CHEF'S NOTE

Yacon syrup is a sweetener you can use on a lectin free diet. It comes from the roots of a yacon plant, which is native to South America. But as usual, use in moderation.

PLANT PARADOX

PHASE 2 & 3 LUNCH

ANTI-LECTIN

SWEET POTATO SOUP WITH COCONUT

SERVES 2

LUNCH
PHASE
2
RECIPES

Ingredients

- 1 tbsp avocado oil
- 1 onion, diced
- 3 small sweet potatoes, peeled and diced
- 450ml/15½floz vegetable stock
- 1 tsp salt
- 1 large pinch of cayenne pepper
- 1 tbsp coconut yoghurt
- Small bunch of coriander, chopped

Method

1 Heat the oil in a saucepan and add the onions. Cook over a medium heat until softened.

2 Add the sweet potato and briefly cook for 1-2 minutes.

3 Pour on the stock and simmer for 10-15 minutes until the potato is cooked.

4 Add the salt and cayenne.

5 Using a stick blender, process until really smooth.

6 Stir through the herbs and yoghurt

CHEF'S NOTE

Cayenne is safe to eat on a lectin free diet as the process of drying and turning the peppers into a powder removes the lectins.

SERVES 1

BOILED EGGS AND "SOLDIERS"

LUNCH
PHASE 2
RECIPES

Ingredients

- 2 eggs – room temperature
- 4-5 spears of asparagus
- Pinch of salt

Method

1 Heat a saucepan of water up until it reaches a boil.

2 Add the eggs one at a time, carefully.

3 Simmer for 7 minutes.

4 Meanwhile, griddle the asparagus and season with the salt.

5 Serve the eggs in egg cups, tops removed ready to dunk in the asparagus.

CHEF'S NOTE

Always use pastured or omega-3 eggs. You should avoid animal and dairy products that have been fed on corn, as this will affect the product.

SERVES 1

HEMP TOFU HASH

LUNCH
PHASE
2
RECIPES

Ingredients

- 1 tbsp avocado oil
- 1 small red onion, halved and sliced
- 2 sticks of celery, sliced
- 125g/4oz hemp tofu (you could make your own)
- 1 tbsp coconut flour
- 1 tbsp nutritional yeast
- 1 tsp salt
- 1 tsp paprika
- 1 tbsp fresh flat leaf parsley, chopped

Method

1 Cut the tofu in to cubes. Mix the flour, nutritional yeast, paprika and salt together and place on a plate.

2 Add the tofu cubes to the mix and stir them around to coat.

3 Heat the oil in a large frying pan and add the tofu. Keep cooking and stirring until it's golden brown and crispy.

4 Add the red onions and celery and stir for 4-5 minutes until they are softened.

5 Remove from the heat and stir through the parsley.

CHEF'S NOTE

Hemp tofu is not made from soy products and is great source of protein if you are a vegetarian or vegans eliminating lectins from your diet.

SERVES 1

AVOCADO SKEWERS

LUNCH
PHASE 2
RECIPES

Ingredients

- 1 avocado, stone removed and diced in to large pieces
- 4 chestnut mushrooms, halved
- 6 basil leaves
- 6 olives, green or black
- 1 tbsp avocado oil
- 1 tbsp dried oregano
- 1 tsp lemon zest

Method

1 Thread the vegetables and olives on to a wooden skewer, alternating them.

2 Mix the oil, lemon zest and oregano together and drizzle over the skewer.

3 Serve immediately.

CHEF'S NOTE

You can eat up to 1 avocado a day on a lectin free diet. They are full of dietary fibre and contain the heart healthy monounsaturated good fat!

SERVES 2-3

BAKED WHOLE CAULIFLOWER

LUNCH PHASE 2 RECIPES

Ingredients

- 1 medium head of cauliflower
- 2 tbsp ghee
- 1 clove of garlic crushed
- ½ tsp ground cinnamon
- 1 tsp cumin
- 1 tsp salt
- 1 tsp paprika

Method

1 Pre-heat the oven to 180°C/Gas Mark 5 and grease a baking tray.

2 Trim the leaves off the cauliflower and cut across the stem underneath so it will sit evenly on the baking tray.

3 Mix the ghee with all of the other ingredients and pour over the top of the cauliflower.

4 Bake for 20-25 minutes until the top is golden and the cauliflower softened.

5 Serve in slices with a little more of the spiced butter if you wish.

CHEF'S NOTE

Cauliflower is a cruciferous vegetable and contains vitamins C, K and B complex. It is a great substitute for potato and rice and can be eaten raw, cooked or pickled.

SERVES 2

FENNEL AND GOATS CHEESE BAKE

LUNCH
PHASE
2
RECIPES

Ingredients

- 1 tbsp avocado oil
- 1 tsp dried oregano
- 1 fennel, root removed and sliced
- 1 small leek, sliced
- 75g/3oz soft goats cheese

Method

1 Pre-heat the oven to 180°C/Gas Mark 5 and grease a baking dish.

2 Place the fennel, leek and goat's cheese in the baking dish and drizzle over the oil.

3 Sprinkle over the dried oregano and bake in the oven for 20 minutes until the cheese is golden and the vegetables cooked.

CHEF'S NOTE

Fennel can be eaten on any phase of the Lectin Free Diet and is a great source of dietary fibre.

SERVES 2

ROASTED HEIRLOOM TOMATOES & MOZZARELLA

LUNCH
PHASE
3
RECIPES

Ingredients

- 4 heirloom tomatoes
- 1 ball of buffalo mozzarella, thickly sliced
- 4-5 basil leaves
- ½ red onion, sliced
- 1 tbsp olive oil
- 1 garlic clove

Method

1 Pre-heat the oven to 180°C/Gas Mark 5 and grease a baking dish.

2 Bring a saucepan of water to a boil. Cut an "X" at the bottom of the tomatoes, just through the skin. Place them in the boiling water for 30 seconds. Peel the skin off, slice and remove the seeds. Chop a little.

3 Alternate a pattern of basil, onion, cheese and chopped tomato around the bottom of the dish.

4 Mix the oil and garlic together and drizzle over the top.

5 Bake in the oven for 10 minutes until melted and softened.

CHEF'S NOTE

When on Phase 3, you can introduce these tomatoes gradually, to check if there are any effects on you, but do not eat the skin or seeds.

SERVES 2

COURGETTE AND MINT SOUP

LUNCH
PHASE
3
RECIPES

Ingredients

- 1 tbsp olive Oil
- 1 onion, diced
- 1 garlic clove, diced
- 1 stick of celery, diced
- 3 medium courgettes, peeled
- Small bunch of fresh mint leaves
- 600ml/1 pint of vegetable stock
- 1 tsp salt
- Coconut or goat's yoghurt to serve

Method

1 Heat the oil in a saucepan and add the onion and garlic. Stir over a medium heat for 4-5 minutes until softened.

2 Add the celery and courgette and cook for a further 5-6 minutes.

3 Add the stock, salt and mint and simmer for 15 minutes until all of the vegetables are soft.

4 Using a stick blender, process until smooth.

5 Add a spoonful of yoghurt and extra mint leaves too if you wish.

CHEF'S NOTE

Courgette is another vegetable that can be re-introduced once at Phrase 3. It is a great anti-oxidant and provides a source of vitamin C.

SERVES 2

CREAM OF MUSHROOM SOUP

LUNCH PHASE 3 RECIPES

Ingredients

- 1 tbsp olive oil
- 1 onion, diced
- 1 garlic clove, diced
- 1 stick of celery, diced
- 1 tsp dried thyme
- 250g/9oz chestnut mushrooms
- 600ml/1 pint of vegetable stock
- 100ml/3½floz organic sour cream (from A2 cows)

Method

1. Heat the oil in a saucepan and add the onion and garlic. Stir over a medium heat for 4-5 minutes until softened.
2. Add the celery and cook for a further 5-6 minutes.
3. Add the mushrooms and thyme and cook until the water starts to evaporate from the mushrooms.
4. Add the stock and salt and cook for a further 10 minutes until the vegetables are all soft.
5. Using a stick blender, process until smooth.
6. Stir in the sour cream.

CHEF'S NOTE

You can use dairy products like this sour cream if they are from animals free of the casein A-1 mutation.

SERVES 2

CHILLED TOMATO AND OREGANO SOUP

LUNCH
PHASE
3
RECIPES

Ingredients

- 1 tbsp olive oil
- 1 onion, diced
- 1 garlic clove, diced
- 1 celery stick
- 1 small bunch of fresh oregano
- 200g/7oz heirloom tomatoes (skin and seeds removed)
- 600ml/1 pint of vegetable stock
- 1 tsp salt
- Pinch of cayenne pepper

Method

1 Heat the olive oil in a saucepan and add the onion and garlic. Cook over a medium heat until softened, about 5-6 minutes.

2 Add the celery and cook for a further 4-5 minutes.

3 Add the fresh tomatoes to the pan and cook until they are beginning to soften and break up.

4 Pour over the stock, salt, cayenne and oregano bring to a simmer.

5 Using a stick blender process until completely smooth.

6 Place in the fridge overnight for the best result.

7 When serving, chop some more fresh oregano and sprinkle over the top.

CHEF'S NOTE

Oregano is a great flavour to accompany tomatoes. It supplies calcium, manganese and iron to the diet and acts as a great anti-oxidant.

SERVES 1

'SPAGHETTI' WITH PESTO

LUNCH
PHASE
3
RECIPES

Ingredients

- 175g/6oz "Slim Spaghetti"
- 1 tbsp parmigiano-reggiano, grated
- 1 tbsp pine nuts
- 1 small bunch of basil leaves
- 1 tbsp olive oil
- 2 tbsp lemon juice
- 1 tbsp extra of freshly grated parmesan to serve

Method

1 Heat the "slim spaghetti" as per pack instructions. (Slim Spagnetti is a konjac flour based pasta available from most health food shops)

2 Place the parmigiana, pine nuts, basil, oil and lemon on a small processor and blend until smooth.

3 Stir through the pasta.

4 Place on a plate and serve with extra cheese, freshly grated on the top.

CHEF'S NOTE

Pine nuts should be eaten in moderation on a lectin free diet. They contain magnesium, iron and potassium and add a lovely creaminess to pesto.

SERVES 2

MINI MUSHROOM PIZZAS

LUNCH
PHASE
3
RECIPES

Ingredients

- 4 large field mushrooms, stalks removed
- ½ ball of buffalo mozzarella
- 8 fresh basil leaves
- 2 heirloom tomatoes, chopped (skin & seeds removed)
- 2 tbsp homemade pesto (or good quality shop brought)

Method

1 Pre-heat the oven to 200°C/Gas Mark 6 and grease a baking tray.

2 Place the mushrooms, top side down on the baking tray.

3 Place 1 basil leaf on the mushroom, then tear a piece of the mozzarella and place on top.

4 Add some of the tomatoes and continue to mix the ingredients between the 4 mushrooms.

5 Top with a drizzle of the pesto and bake in the oven for 15 minutes until cooked.

CHEF'S NOTE

Buffalo mozzarella is allowed on a lectin free diet as it comes from the water buffalo which is not known to have the casein A-1 mutation.

SERVES 2

BAKED AVOCADO WITH HERBS

LUNCH
PHASE
3
RECIPES

Ingredients

- 2 avocados, stones remove and sliced in half
- 1 tsp olive oil
- 1 red onion, diced
- 1 garlic clove, crushed
- 1 stick of celery, diced
- 4 chestnut mushrooms, diced
- 1 tbsp dried oregano
- 50g/2oz baby spinach leaves
- 3 tbsp freshly grated parmigiana-reggiano

Method

1 Pre-heat the oven to 200°C/Gas Mark 6 and grease a baking tray.

2 Place the avocado halves on the tray, skin down.

3 Heat the oil in a frying pan and add the onion, garlic, celery and mushrooms.

4 Stir over a medium heat for 10 minutes until the vegetables are soft.

5 Add the oregano and spinach leaves and stir until they are wilted.

6 Spoon this on top of the avocados and top with the parmesan cheese.

7 Bake for 7-8 minutes until the tops are golden.

CHEF'S NOTE

Always grate parmigiana-reggiano just before you want to use it, it becomes rather dry and the flavour is not quite so good if stored or bought already grated.

SERVES 2

CHEESEBURGER HASH TOPPER

LUNCH
PHASE
3
RECIPES

Ingredients

- 1 tbsp olive oil
- 1 onion, diced
- 1 garlic clove, crushed
- 250g/9oz minced beef (pasture fed)
- 1 tsp salt
- 2 heirloom tomatoes, seeds and skin removed, diced
- 1 tbsp dried oregano
- ½ ball of buffalo mozzarella
- 2 slices of millet toast to serve

Method

1 Heat the oil in a saucepan and add the onion and garlic. Stir for 4-5 minutes until softened.

2 Add the minced beef to the pan, breaking it up a little.

3 Stir over a high heat until browned and cooked.

4 Add the tomatoes, salt and oregano to the pan and continue to cook until the flavours have combined, and everything cooked.

5 Tear the mozzarella in to small chunks and add to the pan. Briefly stir and then top the mixture on two plates, with the millet toast.

CHEF'S NOTE

Always buy pasture-fed proteins as free-range cattle and poultry are fed on corn and this will affect the meat they produce. Corn should be avoided on a lectin free diet.

SERVES 2

CUCUMBER, RADISH AND PRAWN SALAD

LUNCH PHASE 3 RECIPES

Ingredients

- 6 baby cucumbers, peeled, seeds removed and sliced
- 8 red radishes, end removed and sliced
- 1 celery stalk, sliced
- 100g/3½oz watercress, tough stems removed
- 1 baby gem lettuce, shredded
- 150g/5oz cooked prawns
- 1 lemon, juice and zest
- 2 tbsp olive oil
- 1 tsp white wine vinegar
- 1 tbsp toasted sesame seeds

Method

1 Place the lettuce, watercress, celery, radishes and cucumbers into two bowls.

2 Add the prawns to the top.

3 Mix the lemon juice and zest, vinegar and oil together and drizzle over.

4 Serve immediately.

CHEF'S NOTE

Cucumber should be introduced carefully at Phase 3 of the lectin free diet. If there are no affects, this can be added back to your food choices.

PLANT PARADOX

PHASE 2 & 3 DINNER

ANTI-LECTIN

SERVES 2

SWEET POTATO AND QUORN CRUMBLE

DINNER
PHASE
2
RECIPES

Ingredients

- 1 tbsp avocado oil
- 2 small sweet potatoes, peeled and cubed
- 1 red onion, halved and sliced
- 1 garlic clove, crushed
- 1 tbsp freshly grated ginger root
- 200g/7oz quorn "mince"
- 1 tsp cumin
- ½ tsp turmeric
- 1 tbsp macadamia nuts, chopped
- Small bunch of fresh coriander, chopped

Method

1 Heat the oil in a large saucepan and add the onion, ginger and garlic. Stir over a medium heat for 4-5 minutes until softened.

2 Add the sweet potato and a splash of water.

3 Add the quorn and turn up the heat. Add the spices.

4 Stir for 12-14 minutes until the potato is cooked.

5 Stir through the macadamias and coriander.

6 Divide between 2 plates and add a little extra fresh coriander if you like.

CHEF'S NOTE

Quorn is a product made up of mushroom roots and is deemed a mycoprotein. It has been given a mild flavour to resemble chicken and turkey and comes in various forms, like mince, cutlets and steaks. Be sure to avoid the added egg white versions if you are a vegan.

EGGS AND WEDGES

SERVES 1

DINNER
PHASE
2
RECIPES

Ingredients

- 2 eggs
- 1 large sweet potato
- 1 tsp paprika
- ¼ tsp cumin
- 1 tbsp nutritional yeast
- ½ tsp salt
- 1 tbsp avocado oil
- 1 tbsp flat leaf parsley, chopped

Method

1 Pre-heat the oven to 200°C/Gas Mark 6 and grease a baking tray.

2 Mix the oil with the salt, paprika, cumin and nutritional yeast.

3 Scrub the sweet potato and cut into wedges, leaving the skin on.

4 Toss the oil all over the wedges and add to the baking tray.

5 Place in the oven to bake for 20 minutes, until almost cooked.

6 In the last 10 minutes of cooking, remove the wedges, make two spaces on the tray and crack the eggs in.

7 Return to the oven for 10 minutes and remove when the eggs are set and the wedges cooked.

8 Sprinkle on the parsley and serve.

CHEF'S NOTE

Leaving the skin on the potato in this recipe, increases the dietary fibre and improves gut health.

SERVES 2

BAKED SALMON WITH WATERCRESS SAUCE

DINNER
PHASE
2
RECIPES

Ingredients

- 2 salmon fillets
- 7-8 asparagus spears
- 1 lemon, sliced
- 200g/7oz watercress, tough stalks removed
- 1 tsp salt
- 1 lemon zest, and juice
- 3 spring onions, roughly chopped
- 3 tbsp coconut yoghurt
- Extra lemon to serve

Method

1 Pre-heat the oven to 200°C/Gas Mark 6 and grease a baking tray.

2 Place the asparagus spears on the tray with the lemon slices. Add the salmon to the top.

3 Place in the oven for 15 minutes, until just cooked and flaky.

4 Meanwhile, place the watercress, onion, lemon, salt and sour cream in a blender and process until smooth.

5 Serve the asparagus, salmon and sauce between two plates and some extra lemon if you'd like.

CHEF'S NOTE

When choosing salmon, ensure you are buying wild caught fish as they have not been subject to farming, where size and production affects feed and meat.

SERVES 2

CHINESE PRAWN & RICE SALAD BOWL

DINNER
PHASE
2
RECIPES

Ingredients

- ½ head of cauliflower
- 1 tbsp avocado oil
- 1 tsp coconut aminos
- ½ tsp chinese 5-spice powder
- ¼ Chinese lettuce, shredded
- 2 medium carrots, grated
- 200g/7oz cooked prawns
- 10 radishes, shredded
- 6 spring onions, shredded

Method

1 Place the cauliflower in a blender and process until it resembles rice.

2 Heat the oil in a pan and add the soy sauce and 5-spice powder.

3 Add the cauliflower rice to the pan and stir fry for 5-6 minutes until a little soft and fragrant of the spice. Cool.

4 Mix all of the other ingredients together.

5 When the "rice" is cold, divide between 2 bowls and top with the other ingredients.

CHEF'S NOTE

Cauliflower "rice" is so easy to make and a great fridge standby for a lectin free diet that is packed with vitamins. You can add whatever flavours and textures you like and could create egg fried rice, herbed rice or buttered rice for a number of dishes.

SERVES 2

BROCCOLI KEDGEREE

DINNER
PHASE
2
RECIPES

Ingredients

- 1 tbsp avocado oil
- 1 head of broccoli
- 3 spring onions
- 2 fillets of haddock (smoked if you can find the undyed variety)
- 2 hard boiled eggs, cut in to wedges
- 2 tbsp chopped walnuts
- 1 small bunch of fresh flat leaf parsley, chopped

Method

1 Bring a saucepan of water to a boil and gently poach the fish for 8-10 minutes until it is cooked.

2 Place the broccoli in a blender and process until it resembles rice.

3 Heat the oil in a frying pan and add the broccoli and onion, stirring for 5 minutes to softened.

4 Add the walnuts, parsley egg wedges and the cooked fish and carefully combine.

5 Serve between 2 plates.

CHEF'S NOTE

Avoid the dyed haddock as it contains E-numbers. Quality fish that has been properly smoked does not need bright yellow dyes, you will find it to be a pale yellow/cream hue with a beautifully natural, salty flavour.

SERVES 2

BRUSSELS STIR FRY WITH TEMPEH

DINNER
PHASE
2
RECIPES

Ingredients

- 1 tbsp avocado oil
- 150g/5oz Brussels sprouts, shredded
- 6 spring onions, chopped
- 1 garlic clove, crushed
- ¼ savoy cabbage, shredded
- 125g/4oz tempeh (grain free) cut in to strips
- 1 tbsp orange juice
- 1 tsp orange zest
- 1 tbsp balsamic vinegar
- 1 tbsp sesame seeds

Method

1 Heat the oil in a saucepan. Add the spring onion and garlic and cook over a medium heat for 4-5 minutes until softened.

2 Add the tempeh and stir fry over a high heat for 1-2 minutes.

3 Add the Brussels and cabbage and continue to cook until wilted and soft.

4 Stir in the orange juice, zest, vinegar and sesame seeds.

5 Serve between 2 bowls.

CHEF'S NOTE

Brussels sprouts can have a bit of a bad reputation, but there are some great ways to cook them to get them tasting wonderful. They are full of health benefits and contain vitamins A, C and K and folate and manganese.

SERVES 2

QUORN STUFFED PEPPERS

DINNER
PHASE
3
RECIPES

Ingredients

- 2 red peppers, sliced in half, seeds removed, and skin peeled
- 1 tbsp olive oil
- 1 onion, chopped
- 1 garlic, chopped
- 200g Quorn "mince"
- 1 tsp salt
- 6 chestnut mushrooms, chopped
- ¼ tsp cayenne pepper
- 4 thin slices of buffalo mozzarella

Method

1 Pre-heat the oven to 200°C/Gas Mark 6 and grease a baking tray.

2 Heat the oil in a frying pan and add the onion and garlic. Cook over a medium heat for 5-6 minutes until softened.

3 Add the Quorn mince, salt, cayenne and mushrooms and cook over a high heat for a further 5-6 minutes.

4 Place the 4 pepper halves on the baking tray and fill the centres up with the Quorn mix.

5 Lay a slice of mozzarella over the top and bake for 20-25 minutes until the peppers are soft and the cheese bubbling and golden.

CHEF'S NOTE

As with tomatoes, you can gently introduce peppers back to your diet if there are no affects and make sure you remove the seeds and skin.

BEEF STIR FRY

SERVES 2

DINNER
PHASE
3
RECIPES

Ingredients

- 1 tbsp avocado oil
- 200g beef sirloin, cut into strips (pasture fed)
- ½ head of broccoli, cut into florets
- 1 leek, shredded
- 1 garlic clove, crushed
- 1 stick of celery, chopped
- 200g/7oz spinach
- 1 tbsp coconut aminos
- 1 tbsp white wine vinegar
- 1 tbsp yacon syrup
- 1 tsp Chinese 5-spice powder

Method

1 Heat the oil in a saucepan and add the beef strips. Cook over a high heat until browned.

2 Add the leek, broccoli, celery and garlic and stir fry for a further 5-6 minutes until the vegetables are softened.

3 Add the spinach and stir until wilted.

4 Mix the soy, yacon, vinegar and 5-spice together and add to the pan.

5 Cook for a further 2-3 minutes and serve.

CHEF'S NOTE

You can use any vinegar on Phase 3 but you need to ensure they don't contain added sugar.

SERVES 2

SPINACH SORGHUM "DAHL"

DINNER
PHASE 3
RECIPES

Ingredients

- 1 tbsp olive oil
- 1 tsp grated fresh ginger root
- 2 onions
- 1 tsp ground cumin
- 1 tsp ground coriander
- ½ tsp ground cinnamon
- ½ tsp paprika
- 1 tsp stevia
- 80g sorghum, uncooked
- 500ml/16floz vegetable stock
- 1 tsp salt
- 250g/9oz spinach leaves
- 150g/5oz kale, shredded
- Small bunch of coriander, chopped

Method

1 Heat the oil in a large pan and add the ginger, onion and garlic. Stir for 4-5 minutes to softened.

2 Add the spices, the sorghum and stock. Bring to a boil, cover and simmer for 50-60 minutes until the stock has been absorbed and the sorghum is cooked.

3 Add the spinach, kale and salt and stir until wilted.

4 Serve between two bowls with the coriander on top.

CHEF'S NOTE

Sorghum is allowed in moderation on a lectin free diet. It is one of only 2 grains (millet being the other) that has no hull, and therefore no lectins.

SERVES 2

ITALIAN MUSHROOM HOT POT

DINNER
PHASE
3
RECIPES

Ingredients

- 300g chestnut mushrooms, sliced
- 1 red onion, halved and sliced
- 1 fennel, bulb removed, thinly sliced
- 6-7 basil leaves, shredded
- 1 lemon, juice and zest
- 1 tbsp olive oil
- 1 garlic clove, crushed
- 7 black or green olives
- 150g/5oz rocket
- ½ ball of buffalo or goat's mozzarella
- 1 tbsp pine nuts

Method

1 Mix the mushrooms, onion, basil, fennel and rocket together and divide between two bowls.

2 Chop the olives and mix with the olive oil, lemon juice and garlic.

3 Tear the cheese and divide between the bowls.

4 Drizzle over the oil and the scatter over the pine nuts.

CHEF'S NOTE

Olives are an excellent source of vitamin E and iron, good for hormone balancing and blood health.

SERVES 2

MILLET EGG "FRIED RICE"

DINNER
PHASE
3
RECIPES

Ingredients

- 1 tbsp olive oil
- 6 spring onions, chopped
- 1 garlic clove, crushed
- 125g/4oz cooked millet
- 1 bok choi, sliced
- ½ tsp Chinese 5-spice powder
- 1 tbsp coconut aminos
- 3 tbsp chopped fresh parsley
- 250g/9oz kale, shredded
- 2 eggs, beaten
- 1 tbsp sesame seeds, toasted

Method

1 Heat the oil in a wok or large saucepan. Add the spring onions and garlic and cook over a medium heat for 1-2 minutes.

2 Add the cooked millet, bok choi, 5-spice powder, coconut aminos, parsley and kale and stir for 4-5 minutes.

3 Pour the beaten eggs over the top and keep on stirring so it coats the millet and cooks in the pan.

4 Divide between 2 plates and top with the toasted sesame seeds.

CHEF'S NOTE

Coconut aminos is made from coconut sap. It tastes a little like soy sauce so is a great alternative if you are needing to avoid soy and gluten.

SERVES 2

MOROCCAN SALAD

DINNER
PHASE
3
RECIPES

Ingredients

- 1 avocado, stone removed, peeled and sliced
- 100g cooked sorghum, cooled
- 140g/4½oz baby spinach
- 2 fresh apricots
- 2 tbsp flaked almonds
- 1 lemon, juice and zest
- 1 tbsp avocado oil
- Small bunch of coriander, chopped
- 1 tsp cumin
- ½ tsp ground cinnamon

Method

1 Shred the spinach.

2 De-stone and slice the apricots

3 Whisk the lemon, juice, zest, avocado oil, cumin, cinnamon together.

4 Toss all of the salad ingredients together and drizzle over the oil.

CHEF'S NOTE

Fresh apricots contain vitamins A and E and also provide a good source of beta-carotene, which acts as a great anti-oxidant.

SERVES 1

CHICKEN 'RISOTTO'

DINNER
PHASE
3
RECIPES

Ingredients

- 1 head of cauliflower (processed to create "rice")
- 2 chicken breasts, cooked and shredded
- 1 tbsp olive oil
- 1 onion
- 1 garlic clove, crushed
- 3 tbsp fresh sage, chopped
- 200ml/7floz vegetable stock
- 1 tbsp arrowroot
- 1x 14oz tin of coconut cream
- 1 tsp salt
- 1 tbsp nutritional yeast

Method

1 Heat the oil in a large frying pan and add the onion and garlic. Cook over a medium heat for 4-5 minutes until soft.

2 Add the cauliflower rice to the pan with the chicken breast and sage and stir for 3-4 minutes to heat through.

3 Add the arrowroot and stir to coat everything.

4 Pour the stock in to the pan and simmer for 2-3 minutes until thickened.

5 Stir in the coconut cream, salt and nutritional yeast.

6 Serve immediately.

CHEF'S NOTE

This is a great anti-lectin way to still make a comforting bowl of risotto. You could replace the chicken with mushrooms, alter the herbs or add a piece of grilled fish on top.

SERVES 2

OVEN BAKED HERB CHICKEN AND MASH

DINNER
PHASE
3
RECIPES

Ingredients

- 3 parsnips
- 2 sweet potatoes
- 1 tbsp Italian butter
- 1 tsp salt
- 3 tbsp chopped chives
- 4 small chicken thighs, skin removed
- 2 tbsp Italian butter, softened
- Coconut milk to adjust consistency you prefer)
- 1 garlic clove, crushed
- 2 tbsp fresh oregano leaves, chopped
- 2 tbsp fresh thyme leaves, chopped
- 1 tsp rosemary leaves
- ½ tsp salt
- Steamed broccoli to serve

Method

1 Pre-heat the oven to 200°C/Gas Mark 6 and grease a small baking dish.

2 Peel and cube the parsnips and potatoes and place in a saucepan of

3 boiling water for 15 minutes.

4 Meanwhile, mix the softened butter with herbs, garlic and salt and spread over the chicken thighs. Bake for 35-40 minutes until cooked and golden.

5 Drain the water from the vegetables and mash well with the butter and chives. Add a little milk if you would like the mash to be a little thinner.

6 Serve the chicken on top of the mash with any juices left in the dish. Add the steamed broccoli to the plates and serve.

CHEF'S NOTE

This mash is full of vitamins B6, C, E and K and also provides a good amount of dietary fibre, essential for gut health.

SERVES 2

MUSTARD TOPPED HALIBUT AND GREENS

DINNER
PHASE
3
RECIPES

Ingredients

- 1 tsp olive oil
- 1 garlic clove
- 3 tbsp hemp seed
- 1 tbsp Dijon mustard
- 1 tbsp almond flour
- 1 tbsp olive oil
- 2 tbsp flat leaf parsley, chopped
- 2 halibut steaks
- Steamed mix of cabbage and kale to serve

Method

1 Pre-heat the oven to 200°C/Gas Mark 6 and grease a baking tray.

2 Place the haddock fillets on the tray.

3 Mix the hemp seed, mustard, flour, oil and parsley together and spread onto the fish to make a thick coating.

4 Bake for 15-20 minutes until crusty on top and cooked through.

5 Serve on top of the steamed greens.

CHEF'S NOTE

Use Alaskan halibut if possible for this dish, or substitute with another sustainable firm white fish.

PLANT PARADOX

PHASE 2 & 3 DESSERT

ANTI-LECTIN

SERVES 2

AUTUMN FRUIT PLATTER WITH WALNUT CRUNCH

DESSERTS
PHASE
2
RECIPES

Ingredients

- 2 pears
- 2 apples
- 2 figs, sliced
- ½ tsp ground cinnamon
- 2 tbsp walnuts, chopped
- 1 tsp yacon syrup

Method

1 Destone and slice the pears.

2 Core and slice the apples.

3 Divide the fruits between two plates, spreading out in a fan and layering to form a pattern.

4 Mix the syrup with the cinnamon and chopped walnuts and scatter on top of the fruit display.

CHEF'S NOTE

Walnuts are a good source of omega-3 fats and contain iron, calcium, vitamin E and some B Vitamins too.

SERVES 2

LIME AND COCONUT ICE CREAM

DESSERTS **PHASE 2** RECIPES

Ingredients

- 1 avocado, stone removed and peeled
- 1x 14oz tin of coconut cream
- 2 limes, juice and zest
- 1 tsp yacon syrup
- 3 tbsp flaked coconut, toasted

Method

1 Put the avocado in a blender with the coconut cream and lime juice and zest. Process until smooth.

2 Add to an ice cream maker bowl and churn until frozen. Alternatively, you could freeze this in a plastic container and stir through well after two hours to break down the ice crystals.

3 Leave to soften in the fridge for 20 minutes before scooping out and serving with the coconut flakes.

CHEF'S NOTE

Making ice cream like this is much easier and provides the wealth of nutrition from the avocado and coconut without added processed sugars.

SERVES 4-5

STRAWBERRY SHORTCAKE

DESSERTS
PHASE
2
RECIPES

Ingredients

For the shortcake:

- 3 eggs
- 120ml/4floz coconut cream
- 6 tbsp softened French or Italian butter
- 3 tbsp stevia
- 75g/3oz coconut flour
- 75g/3oz almond flour
- 3 tbsp arrowroot
- 1 tsp vanilla extract
- 1 tsp baking powder

Topping

- 125g/4oz strawberries, hulled and halved
- 250ml/8½floz coconut yoghurt
- 2 tsp yacon syrup
- ½ tsp vanilla extract

Method

1 Pre-heat the oven to 180°C/Gas Mark 5 and grease a baking tray.

2 Mix the eggs, coconut cream, butter with the stevia and beat well.

3 Add the flours, vanilla and baking powder and mix well.

4 Shape the dough into a rough "round shaped" with a spatula and bake in the oven for 20 minutes, until risen and golden.

5 Remove from the oven and cool completely.

6 Mix the yoghurt, syrup and extract together and spread over the top of the shortcake.

7 Top with the strawberries and serve.

CHEF'S NOTE

Use Italian or French butter and dairy products as the cows there are free of the casein A-1 mutation.

SERVES 3-4

CHOCOLATE MOUSSE AND RASPBERRIES

Ingredients

- 2 avocados, stone removed and peeled
- 3 tbsp cocoa powder
- 1 tbsp coconut milk
- 1 tsp yacon syrup
- 1 tsp vanilla extract
- 3 tbsp raspberries

Method

1 Place all the ingredients (except the raspberries) into a blender.

2 Process until everything is really smooth.

3 Divide between 3-4 ramekins or pretty glasses and top with the raspberries.

CHEF'S NOTE

Make sure you are using the plain cocoa powder that has no added sweeteners. You want to avoid the Dutch pressed variety as it's an alkalised powder, whereas the plain one is natural.

SERVES 2

CARIBBEAN MOUSSE AND PASSIONFRUIT SYRUP

DESSERTS
PHASE
2
RECIPES

Ingredients

- 2 avocados, stone removed and peeled
- 1 tbsp coconut milk
- 1 tsp yacon syrup
- 1 peach, stone removed peeled and cubed

For The Syrup

- 2 passion fruit
- 1 tsp yacon syrup

Method

1 Place everything (except the syrup ingredients) into a blender and process until really smooth.

2 Mix the passion fruit and yacon syrup.

3 Divide between 2 ramekins and top with the passion fruit mix.

CHEF'S NOTE

Passion fruit is a great ingredient to boost your immune fighting levels. It contains high levels of vitamin C and iron.

SERVES 4

SKINNY CHURROS WITH A CHOCOLATE CREAM

DESSERTS
PHASE
2
RECIPES

Ingredients

- 100g/3½oz tapioca flour
- 1 tsp baking powder
- 2 tbsp avocado oil
- 2 eggs, beaten
- 2 tbsp stevia
- 75g/3oz dark chocolate (at least 72% cocoa)
- 75ml/2½floz coconut cream
- 4 tbsp avocado oil

Method

1 Whisk the flour, oil, eggs and stevia together until smooth.

2 Heat the avocado oil in a saucepan until it reaches 350°F/170°C.

3 Place the flour mix into a small freezer bag and cut off the corner.

4 Squeeze long threads of the mix into the hot oil and cook for 4-5 minutes until golden.

5 Drain on a kitchen towel.

6 Melt the chocolate in a glass bowl over a simmering pan of water. Stir in the coconut cream.

7 Pour the chocolate sauce into a dipping bowl and serve in the middle of table with the skinny churros, for everyone to get stuck in to.

CHEF'S NOTE

When using chocolate for a lectin free diet, make sure you use bars that are at least 72% cocoa and unsweetened. Desserts and baking using this should be reserved for treats.

SERVES 3-4

PISTACHIO ICE CREAM WITH MINT RIPPLE

DESSERTS
PHASE
2
RECIPES

Ingredients

- 1 avocado, stone removed and peeled
- 1x 14oz tin of coconut cream
- 4 tbsp pistachios, chopped
- 1 tsp yacon syrup

Mint Ripple

- 9-10 mint leaves
- 3 tsp yacon syrup
- 4 tsp water

Method

1 Put the avocado in a blender with the coconut cream and process until smooth.

2 Stir through the chopped pistachios.

3 Heat the yacon syrup and water together and add the mint leaves. Simmer for 9-10 minutes and then blend until smooth.

4 Add the ice cream mix to an ice cream maker bowl and churn until quite stiff. Alternatively, you could freeze this in a plastic container and stir through well after two hours to break down the ice crystals. Both methods can have the mint ripple stirred through the ice cream mix as it starts to harden.

5 Leave to soften in the fridge for 20 minutes before scooping out and serving with a sprig of mint on top.

CHEF'S NOTE

Mint is a herb known to help ease stomach complaints and can work as an anti-inflammatory for congestion due to coughs and colds.

SERVES 2

CHERRY AND ALMOND ICE

DESSERTS
PHASE
2
RECIPES

Ingredients

- 200g/7oz frozen cherries
- 2 tbsp almond butter
- 2 tbsp almond milk, unsweetened
- 2 tsp yacon syrup
- 2 tbsp flaked almonds, toasted, to serve

(only use blanched or Marcona almonds as the skin or peel of almonds are high in lectins)

Method

1 Place the cherries, butter, syrup and milk in to a high-speed blender and process until smooth and creamy.

2 Divide between 2 glass bowls and scatter over the flaked almonds.

CHEF'S NOTE

Cherries contain a small amount of quercetin, which is one of the most potent compounds for anti-oxidant processes.

SERVES 8-10

BLUEBERRY AND HAZELNUT GALETTE

DESSERTS **PHASE 3** RECIPES

Ingredients

Filling
- 450g/16oz fresh blueberries
- Lemon juice and zest
- 2 tbsp honey
- 2 tsp tapioca flour
- 150g/5oz almond flour
- 50g/2oz tapioca flour
- 6 tablespoons of Italian or French butter, cubed
- 1 egg, beaten
- 3 tbsp chopped hazelnuts
- 1 egg, beaten for egg wash

Method

1 Pre-heat the oven to 200°C/Gas Mark 6 and grease a small baking tray.

2 In a bowl, rub the flours together with the butter until it resembles fine breadcrumbs. Add the beaten egg and enough water to create a dough.

3 Place the dough in the fridge until it hardens a bit more, for about an hour.

4 When ready to cook, roll out the pastry into a circle, about ½ cm thick.

5 Put the blueberries, lemon juice and zest, honey, tapioca flour in a bowl and mix together well.

6 Tip the blueberries into the centre of the pastry, leaving about a 3cm border.

7 Pull the border up and over the blueberries a little.

8 Brush the egg wash all over the pastry edge and scatter on the hazelnuts, all over the top and the pastry.

9 Bake for 20-25 minutes until the pastry is crisp and golden and the blueberries are oozing.

CHEF'S NOTE

Don't get confused by tapioca flour/starch and cassava flour. They are both from the yucca tuber but are produced in a different way from one another and can't really be substituted.

SERVES 1

COCONUT TAPIOCA PUDDING

DESSERTS
PHASE
3
RECIPES

Ingredients

- 300ml/10½floz A2 specific cow's milk
- 1 tsp vanilla
- 1x 14oz tin coconut cream
- 60g/2½oz tapioca flour
- 3 tbsp yacon syrup
- 4 egg yolks
- 2 tbsp ghee
- 3 tbsp flaked coconut chopped

Method

1 Whisk all of the ingredients together in a saucepan and heat.

2 Cook for 10-15 minutes, cooking continually until thickened.

3 Strain through a sieve and pour into 4 ramekins.

4 Place in the fridge, covered until set.

5 Serve with the flaked coconut on top.

CHEF'S NOTE

A2 cows milk is allowed at Phase 3 of a lectin free diet and is readily available in shops nowadays.

MAKES 9

CHOCOLATE AND MACADAMIA BROWNIES

DESSERTS
PHASE
3
RECIPES

Ingredients

- 1 medium sweet potato, peeled and grated
- 2 eggs, beaten
- 2 tsp vanilla extract
- 5 tbsp yacon syrup
- 120ml/4floz coconut oil
- 1 tsp baking powder
- 75g/3oz cocoa powder
- 2 tbsp almond flour
- 4 tbsp chopped macadamias

Method

1 Pre-heat the oven to 200°C/Gas Mark and grease or line an 8"x8" square baking tin.

2 Beat the eggs, grated potato, vanilla, syrup and oil together until well combined.

3 Mix the baking powder, cocoa powder, almond flour and nuts together with the egg mix and pour into the tin.

4 Bake for 20-25 minutes until the brownies are beginning to shrink in from the side and just set on top. You don't want to over-cook these and the more squidgy they are the better!

CHEF'S NOTE

This should be saved for special occasions as the sugar content is quite high. You could substitute the nuts for a different favourite or leave them out all together.

SERVES 5-6

LEMON AND LIME ICED PARFAIT

DESSERTS PHASE 3 RECIPES

Ingredients

- 1 lemon, juice and zest
- 1 lime, juice and zest
- 300ml/10½floz organic double cream (Guernsey)
- 2x 14oz tin of coconut cream
- 3 tbsp Erythritol (Powder)
- 125g/4oz pecans, chopped
- Lemon and lime zest to decorate

Method

1. Whisk the lemon and lime zest and juice, double cream, coconut cream and erythritol together until really smooth.
2. Line a loaf tin and pour the mix in.
3. Place in the freezer overnight.
4. When ready to serve, remove from the freezer half an hour before and leave in the fridge to soften.
5. Slice into 5-6 pieces and serve with a scattering of pecans and extra lemon and lime zest.

CHEF'S NOTE

This dessert is certainly for special occasions and a great dinner party pudding. Using organic dairy products from Guernsey cows ensures you are eliminating the casein A1 mutation from the foods you consume.

SERVES 2

BLACKBERRY AND HAZELNUT CRUMBLE

DESSERTS
PHASE
3
RECIPES

Ingredients

- 300g/11oz blackberries
- 2 tbsp yacon syrup
- 2 tbsp coconut flour
- ½ tsp ground ginger
- ½ tsp cinnamon
- 3 tbsp coconut sugar
- 2 tbsp almond flour
- 2 tbsp tapioca flour
- 2 tbsp chopped hazelnuts
- 75g/3oz Italian or French butter, cold and cubed
- Coconut yoghurt to serve

Method

1. Pre-heat the oven to 200°C/Gas Mark 6 and grease a medium baking dish.
2. Place the blackberries and syrup on the bottom of the dish and mix together well.
3. In a bowl, add the flours, spices, sugar, nuts and butter and rub together to create a crumbly mix.
4. Tip over the top of the blackberries and bake in the oven for 20-25 minutes until crisp on top.
5. Serve with a coconut yoghurt.

CHEF'S NOTE

Blackberries are great source of Vitamin C and also provide both soluble and insoluble fibre which are essential for a healthy gut.

SERVES 2-3

TAPIOCA CREPES WITH A TOFFEE DRIZZLE

DESSERTS PHASE 3 RECIPES

Ingredients

- 150g/5oz tapioca flour
- 2 eggs
- 400ml/14floz almond milk/coconut milk
- 1 tbsp yacon syrup
- 1 tbsp olive oil
- 10 medjool dates, chopped
- 8 tbsp water

Method

1 Place the dates and water in a small saucepan and bring to a boil. Heat until the dates become pulpy and you are able to use a stick blender to make a thick, sticky syrup.

2 Beat the flour, eggs, milk and syrup together to form a smooth batter.

3 Heat the olive oil in a crepe pan or large frying pan and create a large, flat pancake with the batter.

4 Cook from 1-2 minutes and remove and keep warm whilst you cook the rest of the batter.

5 Serve on plates with the "toffee drizzle" from the dates.

CHEF'S NOTE

Using medjool dates here will ensure you get the juiciest and plumpest dates available, that are full of dietary fibre, potassium, manganese, copper and vitamins A and B.

SERVES 3

GREEN FRUIT ICE CREAM

DESSERTS
PHASE
3
RECIPES

Ingredients

- 2 green bananas, chopped and frozen
- 1 avocado, stone removed, peeled, sliced and frozen
- 2 kiwis, peeled and slices frozen
- 3 tbsp coconut yoghurt
- Chopped pistachios to serve

Method

1. Add the ingredients into a high-speed blender and process until a thick ice cream is formed.
2. You can place the mix in the freezer if you would like it a little more frozen.
3. Divide scoops between 3 bowls and add the chopped pistachios to the top.

CHEF'S NOTE

Green bananas and fruit are allowed on an anti-lectin diet as the sugar content is much lower before the fruit fully ripens.

PLANT PARADOX

PHASE 2 & 3 SNACKS

ANTI-LECTIN

SERVES 1

BLUEBERRY AND MINT LEMONADE

DRINKS
PHASE 2
RECIPES

Ingredients

- 6 fresh mint leaves
- 100g/3½oz blueberries
- 2 tbsp lemon juice
- 2 tsp yacon syrup
- 250ml/8floz sparkling mineral water

Method

1 Place the blueberries, lemon juice, yacon and mint into a high-speed blender.

2 Process until smooth.

3 Pour into the bottom of a glass and top up with the mineral water. Stir and serve.

CHEF'S NOTE

You could change the mineral water to coconut water if you want a "still" drink.

SERVES 1

LEMON HERB SMOOTHIE

DRINKS
PHASE
2
RECIPES

Ingredients

- 1 small avocado, stone removed, peeled and frozen
- 250ml/8½floz skimmed milk or almond milk
- 3-4 ice cubes
- 1 tsp yacon syrup
- 1 tbsp thyme
- 2 tbsp lemon verbena

Method

1. Add all of the ingredients into a high-speed blender.
2. Process until smooth.
3. Serve immediately.

CHEF'S NOTE

Lemon verbena is a great herb to grow in your garden to use in sweet and savoury dishes and drinks.

SERVES 3

ROASTED PECAN MILK

DRINKS
PHASE
2
RECIPES

Ingredients

- 200g/7oz pecans, chopped and roasted
- 1 tsp vanilla extract
- ¼ tsp salt
- 750ml/1¼pt water (filtered is best)
- 500ml/17floz water to soak the nuts

Method

1 Place the pecans, vanilla and salt in the 500ml/17floz of water to soak over-night.

2 Rinse and drain them and then add to a high-speed bender. Process until the mix is as smooth as possible.

3 Line a sieve with a cheese cloth and place over a large bowl.

4 Pour the milk through the cheese cloth and leave to drain for 15 minutes.

5 Begin to squeeze the cheese cloth, wringing it hard to remove all of the milk from the nuts and leaving the dry pecan meal (do not through this away! Use in bakes, or as toppings or add to smoothies).

6 Keep repeating the cheese cloth squeezing until you are happy all of the milk has been removed.

7 Store in the fridge for up to 1 week.

CHEF'S NOTE

You could use other nuts and seeds to make milk (try tiger nuts or hemp seeds) and alternate what you eat and drink to improve your gut health.

SERVES 1

RASPBERRY ZINGER

DRINKS PHASE 2 RECIPES

Ingredients

- 150g/5oz raspberries
- 1 tsp inulin/yacon
- 250ml/8½floz coconut water
- 1 tbsp freshly grated ginger
- Ice to serve

Method

1 Add all of the ingredients into a high-speed blender.

2 Process until all of the ingredients are smooth and pour into a chilled glass.

3 Serve with plenty of ice.

CHEF'S NOTE

Ginger is a known anti-oxidant and anti-inflammatory agent. This is a great pick me up if you are feeling a little delicate after a late night.

SERVES 2

HOT CHOCOLATE

DRINKS
PHASE 2
RECIPES

Ingredients

- 400ml/14floz coconut milk
- 3 tbsp raw cacao powder
- 1 tsp arrowroot powder
- ½ tsp ground cinnamon
- 2 tsp yacon syrup

Method

1 Add all of the ingredients into a small saucepan.

2 Heat gently and bring to a boil.

3 Simmer for 4-5 minutes, whisking continually until thickened.

4 Pour into 2 heated mugs.

CHEF'S NOTE

Arrowroot is a good alternative to cornflour, which needs to be avoided on a lectin free diet. It is easy to mix and will thicken sauces and drinks and give a glossy finish.

SERVES 1

THE PURPLE ONE

DRINKS
PHASE
2
RECIPES

Ingredients

- 1 small beetroot, peeled and chopped
- 250ml/8½floz coconut water
- ½ an avocado, stone removed and peeled
- 2 medjool dates
- Handful of ice

Method

1 Add all of the ingredients into a high-speed blender and process until really smooth. This may take a while due to the beetroot being quite hard. You could grate the beetroot beforehand if your blender may struggle.

2 Pour into a chilled glass and enjoy immediately.

CHEF'S NOTE

Beetroot and dates both have lots of natural sugars that makes this taste quite sweet. This smoothie has lots of dietary fibre and immune boosting vitamin C.

SERVES 1

CHOCO-MOCHA SHAKE

DRINKS
PHASE
3
RECIPES

Ingredients

- 2 tbsp cocoa powder
- 1 tbsp olive oil
- 200ml/7floz coconut cream
- 100ml/3½floz cold, strong coffee
- 1 tsp yacon syrup

Method

1 Place all of the ingredients into a high-speed blender.

2 Process until everything is smooth.

3 Serve in a chilled glass.

CHEF'S NOTE

Coffee can be consumed on a lectin free diet, in moderation. The olive oil and coconut cream will enhance this shake with some welcome proteins and good fats.

SERVES 1

MINT CHOC CHIP SHAKE

DRINKS
PHASE
3
RECIPES

Ingredients

- 250ml/8½floz coconut milk
- 1 tbsp cocoa powder
- 1 tsp yacon
- 5-6 fresh mint leaves
- Large handful of ice

Method

1 Place all of the ingredients into a high-speed blender.

2 Process until the ingredients are smooth and the ice slushy.

3 Serve with extra mint leaves and a sprinkle of cocoa powder.

CHEF'S NOTE

You could use coconut cream or Guernsey cream instead here to create a shake that is a little more indulgent and thick for a special treat.

SERVES 2

NORI CRISPS

SNACKS
PHASE
3
RECIPES

Ingredients

- 1 tbsp olive oil
- ½ tsp garlic powder
- 2 tbsp sesame seeds
- 8 sheets of nori

Method

1 Pre-heat the oven to 200°C/gas mark 6 and grease a large baking tray.

2 Place the nori sheets on the baking tray. Mix the oil and garlic together and then brush the oil onto the sheets.

3 Sprinkle the sesame seeds evenly all over and then bake for 5-6 minutes until they have crisped up.

4 Cut into wedges/squares and snack on.

CHEF'S NOTE

Dried seaweed is a great addition to a snack repertoire. It is rich in iodine, calcium, magnesium and can be shredded over eggs or salads to increase nutrition.

SERVES 2

GARLIC ROASTED RADISHES

SNACKS
PHASE
3
RECIPES

Ingredients

- 100g red radishes, ends trimmed
- 2 garlic cloves crushed
- 1 tbsp avocado oil
- ½ tsp salt
- 2 tbsp flat leaf parsley, chopped

Method

1 Pre-heat the oven to 200°C/gas mark 6 and grease a large baking tray.

2 Mix the oil, parsley, salt and garlic together.

3 Mix with the radishes and place on the baking tray.

4 Bake for 10-15 minutes until crisp on the outside and soft in the middle.

CHEF'S NOTE

Radishes are packed with vitamins E, A, C, B6 and K. They also contain essential minerals such as magnesium, copper, calcium, iron and manganese.

FIGGY CHEESE

SERVES 2

SNACKS PHASE 3 RECIPES

Ingredients

- 4 ripe figs sliced lengthways
- 75g/3oz goats cheese, sliced thinly
- 2 tbsp lemon juice
- 1 tbsp pomegranate molasses
- 2 tbsp sesame seeds

Method

1 Place the fig slices on to a serving platter. Top each slice with a little piece of goat's cheese.

2 Mix the lemon juice, molasses and seeds together and drizzle over the platter.

3 Serve at room temperature.

CHEF'S NOTE

Pomegranate molasses is a great dressing addition for lectin free dishes. It has a natural sweetness that can be drizzled over many dishes. It is made simply by boiling down pomegranate juice to reduce to a thick syrup and could easily be made yourself.

SERVES 2

SAVOURY GRANOLA

SNACKS PHASE 3 RECIPES

Ingredients

- 1 tbsp pecan, chopped
- 1 tbsp hazelnuts, chopped
- 1 tbsp walnuts, chopped
- 2 tbsp hemp seeds
- 2 tbsp almond flour
- 2 tbsp coconut oil
- ½ tsp smoked paprika
- 1 tbsp nutritional yeast
- ¼ tsp salt

Method

1 Pre-heat the oven to 200°C/Gas Mark 6 and grease a large baking tray.

2 Mix the hemp seeds, flour, oil, paprika and nutritional years together and squeeze to form clumps.

3 Add the nuts to the mix and tip on to the baking tray.

4 Bake for 10 minutes until golden and crunchy.

CHEF'S NOTE

Although high in good fats, such as omega-3 and monounsaturated fats, this should be eaten in moderation. It's perfect to top a salad, soup or other dish with to create some texture.

COCONUT FREEZER CRISPS

SERVES 2

SNACKS
PHASE
3
RECIPES

Ingredients

- 200g coconut yoghurt
- 1 tbsp yacon syrup
- 1 passion fruit
- 1 tbsp black sesame seeds
- 4 tbsp raspberries, chopped and squashed a little
- 4 strawberries, hulled and finely chopped
- 2 tbsp desiccated coconut toasted

Method

1 Line a baking tray with baking paper.

2 Mix the yoghurt and syrup together until smooth.

3 Pour over the baking paper keeping the thickness to 1/2cm.

4 Scatter on all of the other ingredients and swirl through a little, so the raspberries "bleed" a bit into the yoghurt. Halve the passion fruit and drizzle the seeds over the top too.

5 Freeze for 2-3 hours.

6 Break up into crisps and either serve immediately or store in a plastic container in the freezer for up to 2 weeks.

CHEF'S NOTE

Alter the yoghurt to a different lectin free type if you wish and add what seasonal fruits you have. It's a great way to use up ripe fruits so they are stored in the freezer, without going off in the fridge!

98232227R00055

Made in the USA
Lexington, KY
06 September 2018